Passionate Life

E.S. Spotted Bear

AuthorHouse™
1663 Liberty Drive
Bloomington, IN 47403
www.authorhouse.com
Phone: 1-800-839-8640

First published by AuthorHouse 11/30/2009

ISBN: 978-1-4490-4918-8 (sc)

Printed in the United States of America
Bloomington, Indiana

This book is printed on acid-free paper.

I dedicate this book to all my inspirations. I thank you for all the very memorable ups and downs. I shall always be left with an eagerness to continue writing.

Special thanks to Eryn Wallis and Jaxon St. Paul for all your hard work and dedication. This book is a realization of a long-awaited dream because of your efforts.

Mama,

Thank You For Being The Greatest Friend I Could Hope For. My Love For You Is Sure of God Send. Thank You For The Encouragement.

Love You,

E. R.

Contents

Introduction

I first began writing as a therapeutic method to deal with the struggles and the joys of everyday life. It has been a journey to express my thoughts and feelings onto paper. When I discovered the truth of my emotions through reflection, I realized I could overcome anything. I am grateful for these memories and to those who helped me find parts of my true self. I hope these lines encourage and uplift all who read them.

Origins

Alive

Purest of forms, beautiful in nature and elegant in poise is the woman I see before me. Your hair lies ever so gently along your shoulder covering the bosom of womanhood. The look upon your face is graceful beyond compare. Your neckline is slender, inviting to sweetly kiss. Colors of the sky and bursts of sunshine reflect in your eyes. Leave me to stare into a moment of hopeful dreams of this conversation leading to a future of endless joy. Courage has not made the connection to adventure into another sentence of this chance meeting. It doesn't matter that I may not have another opportunity to obey the impulse to leave my heart right where it had fell in love. I cannot deny the innocence that shows love is alive and living within me.

Temptation

Emotions are a valuable possession that can lead to almost any undeniable reaction. An incredible twist of fate can be produced by the smallest of intentions. The littlest wink, the slightest brush against another, or the simplest compliment can be misconstrued. The heart is the source of all emotion to live and breathe. Tampering with love in unintentional lust revolves desire into the outer rim of discrete complexions. The hidden intent is to be as close to the flame without getting burned. In the midst of compromising the soul, the center of being complete remains empty.

Lady

A curious girl with a curious name visited me in a dream. A wondrous sight for all beauty she beheld. Some people thought her too free a spirit; others remembered her for the love that sprang life into everyone who met her. She had a love of many beauties in her world. I had fortune of meeting her while out for a walk. Unusual events seemed to take place whenever around this maiden. I began to encounter indulgences of her revealing secrets to me. I sensed her compassion and relentless endurance for giving. At once, I too began to feel compassion for life and those around me. She began to stir a love inside of me I had never experienced. Her love for me had stroked my senses to know passion for its vivid colors of my world. As I began to spend countless days with her, I found my passion in the depth of my mind's eye. I brought hell toward the light and now this light surpasses the darkness. I am free to begin anew.

Blindsided

I watched as you came from around the corner. I had seen your eyes in a sparkling new light. I asked myself, "Is this the friend I have long desired to hold in my heart?" I can only imagine how it would be to have that someone to talk to about anything and everything. I hope for someone to sit and listen to the continuous ramblings only a friend could endure. I found a passion in the way I look into your eyes. I can hold your hand and everything fades away. Colors seem to surround those eyes and bring such love and desire into the room. I try not to notice you, but for that split second it is too late. Electricity travels up my spine and into my smile. Those around me begin to notice the uplifted spirit that always envelops me. I have realized I am a better woman because of this renewed spirit you have stirred inside me. I can only explain what I feel and what is going through my heart. I have seen the boundaries that can never be crossed, but still I am holding onto love. There is one thing that is unreachable to a woman who yearns for forbidden desires. In a length, I haven't been this alive and I have you to thank. I do not wish to be without the creations I love and neither should I wish to lose what I have found. I only want to keep you, the muse, in my heart and in my mind.

Depth

To what degree will I go to prove how much I am fighting the temptation to give myself over to contemplation? Arouse the senses to enrage the past and move the future into the present. Incredible fears have awakened in the foremost of my heart. Irregular emotions come daily to stifle the air that so freely flows back and forth, back and forth, back and forth into the sweetness of passion. Chills produced by the tingle of your breath on my neck; moist lips licked by the tongue of desire to taste my mouth upon your own; embraced in your warmth as you relax on my chest and caress my hair over and over again. Slowly you find your way to hold my womanhood with delicate comfort, knowing exactly why I am yours and knowing when to bring me to satisfaction. Aligning the kisses softly down my spine to a point of ultimate extraction. Both hands clasped in yours, I have no room to move. Neither shall I attempt to escape the tangled hold of submission. Ending this irrefutable abomination, I cry to heaven. Let it last till my body cannot withstand restoration. I arise swiftly to know it was some damned hallucination.

Pretentious

If I dreamt of a brighter day under the sun, it does not include familiar engagements. I dare to be beneath the voluptuous trees in rich bloom with tasty fruits. I encumber knowing what I have already seen. I reach for the unexplainable and the unfortunate. I bow my head and arch this spine to the exhaling winds of change. Pull the locks of beauty to halter up the grand event in seven-stepped rhythms. I caught a glimpse of you in the shadows as I allowed the moment to overtake my urgency, and I saw the blood stand red in your glare. I held onto the lattice and channeled all my rage toward the light and found nothing left of hatred. Drop your burden of my pleasure as waste and leave me as we met. Ultimately deep-rooted in disbanding a bond to be foretold anymore, waiting to take up where you once held firm. Gather the remains of this day and fertilize the next. I shall grow filled and high. Beauty will be seen for a second time, but not by you.

A Known Peace

Happiness is not a dream to someone who awakens to disappointment and frustration; the cruel reality of being left to soothe self-inflicted wounds from loving an unappreciative soul. Happiness is a fantasy of a life to only be told as bedtime stories to ease the mind. Hoping to find a place where, for a few hours of peace and solitude, all is precious; huddled in the corner of darkness, squeezing every drop of warmth from a ragged scrap of cloth, hanging onto the only security in arms' reach. Sleep softly, dream well in love and remember the happiness. There is not a trace of fear or a hint of loneliness, just a glimpse into tomorrow that all can be changed in the coming light.

Rebirth

Passion has a way of following the seasons. In the winter, I knew our love would fade. January came and went with a drop in temperature and our relationship. Buried beneath the snow and ice, I felt the coldness of your touch. In the most confusing sense I lost the real moments of desire during the winter nights. I yearned for the renewal of the spring. I longed for your kiss. Dripping from the branches were the tears that fell from my caramel eyes. I prayed your heart would melt at the slightest glance from me. I soon felt the warmth of your embrace. A seed had begun to grow. Buds peaked beneath the dead foliage, giving off a sensuous color in a gray and dingy world. We nurtured them with care and soon the blossoms opened and splashed our world with a riot of love.

Writing

Delicate and smooth are the felted fibers of this parchment. Pressed in and of itself, this paper was created to hold a medium that may display my God-given talent. I can feel the silky threads beneath my hand as it outstretches my inner thoughts. The colors of grain and process are the tangents left behind. A process of birth, life, creativity in reflection and ultimately a note well-carried. Fragrances are mailed through the script of love and memories. Faint tears stain the closing sincerity. Who may be so obligated and privileged as to imprint these lines upon the rice paper they had not known? Only time will tell the story meant for a heart to remember.

Search

My love searches for you in the depths of the darkest night.
I hold on to the hope of the rising sun. I stumble around in
the pitch, yearning for guidance. My lungs fill with the
sweetness of the cold, chilled air and I lose the consciousness
I am struggling to obtain. I reach for your hand and give
myself into your comfort. My security is in knowing my
love lives with you. No more solitary nights of tear-soaked
pillows, only the reassurance that you are my life. It is hard
to know that tomorrow is not a guarantee, but the worry
has no place in our world. Love rescues us from the
unknown and places us on top of the discouragement letting
us see what we have left behind. My ray of hope is heard in
the soft music that comes from your soul. I have found my
light and I will bathe in its warmth.

Awaken

Drown

Visions of the day come to me in wild ambitions to overtake my sadness. My soul is set to bring me out of the darkness toward the light. I am wavering in the blue of the mindless abyss. Silently my soul is rescuing itself, as if a lifeguard is dragging my body one-armed toward the surface. I could have swallowed the entire ocean and never thought of thirst again. I would have found solace in making the floor my burial, sunken beneath the reef. I have seen the dead lying below surrounded by the floral of the ocean. I was saved by the compassion within and delivered to another gift of life. I find myself choking and gasping for air on the sandy beach. I stare across the horizon and think, *I almost missed the sunset.*

Mindful Dreams

We lay silently next to one another hoping the other is deep in sleep, and not awakened by the loud churning going on in my mind. My eyes are glossy and I can barely stand the burn. I dare not shut out the thoughts of tonight's cordial mood. I could not remove her from my mind. I lay next to the man that has promised to love and cherish only me. Guilt rips the sheets and tears swell in my eyes. My heart pounds and I can only think of her. I wish time would flow like the river and daybreak would come. Time can no longer be a factor when she is near. Until I see her again I will think of nothing more. Damn the dreams! I want reality and her lying where I now find him.

Beachside

I see you pleasantly at peace with the world around you. I
see the smile in your laughter and the joy in your heart. I
can always look into your eyes and know exactly what your
soul is revealing to me. The plain and awkward truth is that
the love we share is only between the surface of an outside
world and no deeper than wades of tide quickly coming in
and going out. Love is said and even felt to those who walk
close enough to the shore. The refreshing spray of waves
can become masked and perceives as drench after time.
Love is no more than the sprays of time and journey. I
want to be drenched in love from diving into the ocean and
becoming overwhelmed by the sea. Give me breath and
save me from ourselves. Join me hand in hand as we live
deep below the surface of the coral reef. Come to my side
and swim in this ocean of our life and not stand along the
shore anymore.

Hills

There is a small place in the midst of a wooded clearing.
The sun shines straight into the heart of this tranquil grove.
The warmth is felt as soon as one steps into the light.
Everything that is known from reality is lost in the glow
from the sun. I sit and find my moment alone. I can hear
nature speaking to me. I feel the wind blow around me and
through me. I smell the cedar in the air and I am
mesmerized by the aromas nature has to offer. I fall into
meditation and immediately feel at peace in my own
existence. My mind clears of all that has held it in captivity.
I let go of the bondage that holds me in a crowded life. I
seek love in the most peculiar places. I found it only once in
this secluded treasure.

Captive

You command my breath and place your hand over my mouth, then ask me why I do not speak. My touch is yours to feel, but you tie me to your control and ask me why I do not hold you. Our love crushes the atmosphere with a gravity of adoration. You flank my movements and ask me why I do not take you as my own. Give me time and grant me freedom, then I will gladly let my passion flow through every venue you wish to experience.

Bound

Incessantly I am bound by order and possessive entanglements so I cannot see the window of my future. I hold onto the slightest imperfections of my world and expound on making them my greatest attribute. Bring me into a time of genuine passion and freedom to explore love untamed or unbridled by society. Leave me to my fantasy of perfect peace and comfortable embrace. I stand in a moment of pleasure and pain not knowing my love is yet to be discovered. I am seeking you.

Recovery

There is no denying the emotions that are experienced during love, or loss of love. Thoughts flow too fast to grab reality. In the moment of excitement of newly found love, no one cares. It's a free breeze of all things new, waiting to be discovered. When love is taken back, the world stops and nothing else is alive. The hurt, the pain, the emptiness is all that is felt. Then the questions start to come without answers. Who will listen to the questions? Who will care that your heart was broken? Who will help in the mending? Who will love you again? The answers come slowly and gently. Ask and it will be given. Hold on tight and you shall be carried. Give me your tears and you will smile. Love me and love will always be in your life. The sun comes out from behind the clouds and warms the heart. Laughter is heard and hands are held. Hugs are felt and kisses are given. Passion is seen and love is revealed.

Creation

Standing in the sun staring up in the warmth of the day, I feel my soul rise toward heaven. I have an overwhelming sense of peace. I find my vision has been cleansed and I can see all things in a different light. I have released the unrighteousness I have committed. I am no longer the shadow of the woman I used to see. I look forward to meeting a stronger woman, not afraid or timid. I hope I see her in my dream. I hope I recognize her voice when I hear her. I wonder if the beauty will be reflected in the mirror, or if the hideous will remain. I see the elegance in that woman and long to touch her hand and have her guide me in this journey. I have been released from the death I should have experienced. I can see faint images of her now. What will be revealed in the days to come?

My Day

The sun rising in the east bring with it the brightness of new life. I am hopeful to know that each day I am awakened to you I have love in my life. During midday activities that engage us in sensuous embrace, you reveal the tenderness in your kiss. I am stimulated in my soul to rage against all that suppress our joy. As the sun sets softly and quietly, I am holding onto your hand. Gently your look reminds me of the strength we have as one. We smile at all things perfect and every issue less than perfect. Delicately the moon hovers over our dreams. Forgiveness reassures me we have chances to change our indifferences.

Morning Blues

In the rush and confusion of the day the love and desire seems to fade away. The mind gets filled with responsibility and demand. I see the beauty in your eyes and the love in your smile. None of that can penetrate the urgency of another scheduled day. I walk past you as if you weren't there. I see your blue eyes and still I cannot be deterred. You whisper my name to stop my momentum and to slow my hurried thoughts. At first I am taken off guard and I want to scream, but with one gently kiss I am at ease. Your Scottish blues are the downfall to my pride. I have no strength nor can I speak but to ask for another. Take me away with your tender lips and let's start this day again.

Spring Rain

Deep in the night I felt a cold, damp breeze blow in from the west. I heard the faint rumble of thunder. I smelled the sweetness of spring rain in the air. Half asleep I stumbled to close the weather out. I caught a shimmer of light over the hay field. I noticed someone in the midst of the windblown blades. I thought of you and turned to find you were gone from our bed. A chill sped throughout my limbs. I raced down the stairs to the door left wide open. I stepped over the threshold and all the wind and rain had stopped in silence. The moon shone brighter than any other night. Sounds quickly filled the air. Slowly I walked toward you and gently put my hand in yours. I tried to see your expression. I had to know why you chose to leave our warmth and rest. Your eyes met mine and I saw the tears that left their trail down your cheeks. "Why are you here in the dark?" You turned and shook your head with a smile of tenderness. "I wanted to remember our love in the spring."

Thrive

Bedtime

The grey, imperial draperies flow in the wind and create a soothing melody as they brush back and forth against one another. Quite is true about the love you and I share behind the slate drapes. Our song begins as the lights dim and even extinguishes them when the ocean breeze finds its way to our enclosure. The aroma of burnt cedar fills the air and masks the undertone of wax and tempered wood. The coolness of the night is not felt under sheets of Egyptian cotton. A moment of gently stroking the body and making the pain of daily work and tension disappear. I take stock of every inch of your body and caress your backside of natural color. Your beauty hides beneath black waves of hair as you lie on your belly. I am captivated by the soothing touch of your skin. I move slowly over your hamstrings, down beneath your thigh, and up into that heated pool of desire. I tirelessly travel up and down the full length of your torso and never cease to be amazed by the gentle kiss I receive once I have reached my destination. In the twilight of a new day I am renewed and exhausted all in the same rhythm of love. Beyond the drapes and beyond the night I live my dream, strive to perfection, and await the cry to never stop.

Trio

So many images come to flash before my eyes. I see the little girls play in the courtyard and the little boys digging in the sandbox. Innocence brings a smile to my heart, knowing that love, joy and peace are the only concerns for these small children. Wide-eyed, big grins and tussled hair are the portraits I see everyday. Three sweet faces ready to explore a new world. The first is the caring protector, eager to help and always willing to do more. The second is the ever-mobile prankster, always looking for ways to have fun with the biggest grin you'll ever know. The third is quiet and petite. Sure is the smile of her every morning. All three have the energy of the sun, and the radiance of love and sweetness for each other. These are the joys and my everlasting love of life.

Thoughts

Today I heard your voice being carried by the wind. I turned to look and see your image. I caught a swirl of leaves around me. I knew it was you embracing me from afar. The breeze blew upward and lifted my hair as you would if it were in your hands. I closed my eyes and let the air caress my face. Once the moment had passed, I smiled as deep and wide as I ever had before. I hummed a little tune and skipped a sidestep. I loved knowing that somewhere in this big, wide world you were there thinking of me.

Sleep in Rhythm

Bring me to the deep folds of the bed and cover me in the flesh of my love. Create a movement in sensational timing. Breathe in excess and exhale in passion as the Egyptians cover the bed in cotton and stream the walls in lilacs and lavender. I want to feel the fragrances, hear the colors, and taste all I see. Push me past the realm of inevitable experiences and expose me to the truth of what love really means. Examine my thoughts and search your heart. Discover my world intermingling in the night as our heat rises to move us to a state of erotic fantasies. Move in and out of reality as we gain the strength to love once more. Do not listen for the morning to come, keep silent as the daylight forces its way through the lace. Let us close our eyes to the rest of the world and hold onto this moment for another time.

Muse

Turn me on and feel the music as we dance to the beat of our own drum. It's like the passion flows freely around us as the wind swirls between our bodies. Salty, cool breezes refresh the air as mist sprays in from the ocean. It isn't easy to look onto your eyes and not lose my sense of balance. My soul is adjoined to your love and I exuberate nothing but joy. Indescribable desire fills my heart and time cannot hinder these feelings. Thrilling experiences are keeping me from my normal life of routine. How do I make this image vanish of your blue eyes as if looking at sapphire jewels? Keep me from falling over the edge and not returning to everything that was once familiar to me.

Nocturnal

A million stars float above shining so bright. Here we lay
beneath the night and hold each other arm in arm. Down
the country road the sound of dogs barking and howling
brings to mind that life continues after the sunset. The
sycamore owl's *hoo* spins thoughts that we are not alone.
All the music of nature plays a melody to the beat of the
wind. I lie close to you and lose myself in the color of your
look. Our bodies intertwined in passion and desire. The
lullaby of the gentle brook soothes us both to dreams. In
the deepest realms of love I can see the million stars above.

Sings in Her Heart

The heart of a woman is not easily heard in the first beat.
All that is experienced in a single life could never be
revealed in another. A moment of true passion and
complete fullness would take a lifetime to enjoy. The music
that keeps the steps in rhythm moves the fullness of a family.
The song that is sung in the understanding over the flowing
river is refreshed by each cool drink. The wind sways and
the motion carries the love around and around. Strength in
the arms of a woman is felt in the ability to uphold all that is
good, and holds back the evil that tries to overcome it.
Bring me your hurts and I will pray over you; give you
encouragement to keep going. Dance with me and we will
share a life together. Love me and we shall never want for
anything again in our lives.

Playing

Midday comes and passes time by floating clouds and flying birds. The warmth of the sun comforts my mind's eye and I drift to sleep. I dream of the sea and crashing waves. I can taste the salty air and feel the mist across my face. I walk across the beach and feel the sand under my feet, and in between my toes. The sounds of the seagulls flying overhead in their swirling motion soothe the dizzying reality of life. I hum a note or two, dance a step, and spin around. I have lovely thoughts of childhood dreams and little games that pass the days away. Delicate imaginations running free, wishing of the day we grow and find our place. I hop, skip and splash through the ankle-deep waves as they roll in and out. I am in love with these days of my innocent life.

High School Sweetheart

Bright and shining is the sun with all the warmth and joy of
newness. I come to see the festival of love, and I bump into
you. We smile and we greet each other well. Come walk
with me and let us talk awhile. We ramble on about the
highs and lows of life. Most of all, we go on like only
parents can over their children. We begin with the usual
questions that follow suit. How many? How old? Boys?
Girls? We laugh and remember the old school days, and we
can't believe we got away with the adolescence of our
actions. Soon we look and notice the change in our face,
and see time has been kind. Oh! What a joy to see you
now and how wonderful this encounter has made my day.
I leave you sitting on the park bench and I begin to pray
God continues to follow you. I walk into the sun and
remember how much loving you was fun.

Love

Eyes locked in a loving stare and hands grasped in an unbreakable bond. My muscles flexed in grateful pain. I'm holding onto the passionate desire of restraint. I try to push and pull the environment around us. I can hear the water in the wind and taste the moisture in your kiss. Cross the bed and feel our bodies intertwine on the last hope that tomorrow will not disappoint. Quiet yourself and look forward to happiness. Let me do your worrying for you tonight. There is no shame in leaving every burden on the ground, never to be picked up again. Friends come and go, lovers spend the night and dreams fade with the morning light. Only the thread of a heartfelt touch can remain to be seen. Let me cry again and again. Bring the tears of passion with the laughter of your desire.

Sleep

She holds me in the cradle of her arms and I sleep tenderly
in the lofty realms of dreams. My mind swims in the haze
of love, and thoughts flow as free as the lullaby in the air.
The face of an angel watches over me as I deeply slumber.
She is protecting me from the harsh entanglement of the this
cold world. Mindful of the life and the time in which we
live, I try to grasp the reality of our love together in this
new experience of age. Her tender lips place upon my
forehead her care and comfort. The strength in her is the
support I had only desired in a love. I will enjoy this night
for the sun rises soon.

Dance

I feel your hand cross my shoulders and I feel the breath of a kiss on my back. I close my eyes, lean into your arms and wrap myself in your love. The movement of us together, swaying to the music in our moment, kept time to the mood that was beginning. I lost track of time, the place we were in and who might find us enjoying each other. Nothing else matters when I am in your embrace; only the touch, the kiss, the movement, the deep moan of passion is occupying my mind. I slide to your reach and hover in your hands. Keep the timing to the music of my hips and step to my dance. I follow you wherever you may lead.

Indian Summer

In the heat of an afternoon I see you leaning against the front door, hoping for a cool breeze. I stand and stare at the curvatures of your silhouette. A linen dress clings to your chest and flows around your abdomen. Sweat trickles down your neck and beads roll into your top. Slowly, I reach for your hand. Never a startled movement, you are in acceptance of my love, which pulls me closer to you. I see all the tones of cream in your soft skin as it shows through to the sun. Moving to the Latin rhythms in the background, your hands guide my hips to sway in time to yours. Slowly twirl me and step to the side, bring me back into the arms of compassionate tenderness. Together we slide to each beat of poetic verse. We make it across the room and fall upon a cool bed. My back arches in the rise of your arms. Thumping of bass brings me to feel excitement. We find a place to exasperate in the midst of an hour. Perspiring from the weather or extreme passion, I lose sight of what is bringing my blood to heat. Fading out with the song, I stare into your eyes as I fall into relief.

Innate

Beautiful is the reflection of the moon off the rippling lake. The hint of sweetness in the air gives an arousing taste to the lips. I walk closely beside and talk of hilarious travels that could always bring a chuckle. I love to make a smile appear upon your face. We leave the night behind as we close the door to the bedroom. I feel your excitement when I brush the line across your shoulder. The wink in your eye displayed a little grin of orneriness. I wait and watch the clothes fall to the floor. Your back turned to me and I feel as though I am intruding. I close my eyes and turn my cheek. Slowly, I feel your hand guide me to see your smile. I cannot take my eyes off your lips. I caress the suppleness in front of me. I taste the tenderness on top of me. I lose myself in the love given to me. I hear the stimulation in your breathing. I listen to your moans and let them dictate my own pleasure. Time has no meaning in the captive nature of this moment. Only the purpose in our hearts keeps the measure. When the end is near, I shall weep for more. Until that moment, I shall take pleasure in every element of you.

Evanesce

An Afternoon

Kites fly up in the turbulent blue Sky. The Sunshine reflects the hidden colors of the material. We enjoy the vibrant days of running, laughing and play. The green, soft grass cushions our steps and cleans our toes while providing a soft place to rest. We look up at the clouds and blind ourselves by seeking heaven. The day passes, and the wall clouds form, and the Sky darkens. In the distance, the thunder rolls and the smell of Rain is in the air. We pull down the colorful flyers and we pack away our memories. The drops fall and refresh the spring day. We look back to notice there was no sign left behind that we had been there at all, only nature in its purest form.

Hallowed

Not everything is bound by promise, or even by the word of those that lived a thousand years ago. The daily character of a person reaches far more and holds more respect than any ideal that could have been translated for you or I today. I am a school girl whining for the last word of an argument. I beg and plead to live with your love and feel the most intimate part of you. I have been there and it was good. The only destruction to my world is the rejection of someone else's idea for my morality. I feel your love for me and I also feel the refusal to pursue that love you once felt. I bind no words to our love; I only live for what I feel for you. I see the end in a different way; I see that I will answer for my thoughts, my actions and my heart. All of which will be filled with you and our life together. Do not condemn me for being me, and I shall not look twice and disbelieve any life you wish for yourself. I only want to be a part of it and continue to love you in my own way.

Brooke

I hear your thoughts and I can decipher the message within the songs you play for me. I would love to kiss your lips and I can hear you call my name. I want to be your close friend and intimate refuge. I have so much to lose if this doesn't work for more than an uncontrollable urge to hit the line of no return. I would not want to abandon the relationship that has grown into more than a chance meeting. I think of you often and remember the color of sunlight in your hair, the blue in your eyes, and the sweetness of your lips. I realize I am not the security you desire, nor the love that has made you into the woman you are today. I am grateful for the moment I have had in your life. Brush against me one last time. Let me smell the fragrance in your hair and caress your hands in the moonlight of our tomorrows. The babbling Brooke tells me time has run short and my exit is near. Sing me another tune as I close my eyes to your memory.

Laundered

Diligent maiden toiling in the sun, washing the soiled rags against the cold stone of the river's edge. The rush of cool, clear water begins to chill the fingertips. The radiance of heat gives no relief to daily chores of endless ritual. Beauty and grace hide the thoughts and feelings of yearning for a different life. Arranging the clothes for a proper hanging along the drooping line, wondering if another life was offered, would this same task become part of that life? Even flow of the cloth to make sure no wrinkles remained, pinning the next article with attention to detail, the sun shimmers through the thin clothes to show a sculptured body of perfection. The imagination is not left to run wild, only left with certainty. A soft lullaby is hummed as the feet follow in an elegant step to the side, the hips roll to keep in time. A soft gentle breeze begins the drying process, as dark auburn hair blows free from around the defined looks of beauty. All has been accomplished and nothing remains but time.

Apprehensive

Massive quantities of thoughts sway in the mind. The pounding of the heart can be heard ringing through my ears. The pressure of holding you in my arms weighs me down. I try to speak well of you and keep you encouraged, drastically I believe I fail. The thought of having to yell, scream, and get my point across is exhausting in itself. Blatant is the tone I relate to these past few days and nights. Hope keeps me strong and love keeps me sane. The anger I see in you and the rage I feel when you look at me fries my brain. Immediately I find myself standing on eggshells trying not to break a single one. My balance is tipping between ever-loving happiness and creating the monster I am afraid you will become. Creativity is my escape to a world untouched by reality. I pray for silence when I catch that glimpse of you down the block. Sometimes I don't get a busy signal and we are parting in sweet dreams. Count me blessed for I have survived another evening.

My Troubadour

I stare at the road as I walk and remember the days of love and passion I had felt for knowing her, if only for a moment in my life. A tear rolls down my face as the images rush into my mind. I feel every emotion she gave me. Her eyes captivated my heart and left my body yearning for her attention. I lost my thoughts when she looked my direction. I felt silk when she touched my hands. Kissing her became another world in which I lived. Her music will forever be the song to which I dance. So now I drift to sleep accompanied by images of rivers and streams where we had strolled. Places of tall trees and valleys wide of where we laid our love. For the remainder of my dream, I sleep with a smile and in peace.

Intrigued

Beyond the curtain into a dim lit room a silhouette floats closer to my bedside. I can catch the scent of perfumed jasmine and oils wafting in the gentle wind. A slender hand glides across the silk sheets reaching for my own. I lay silent and motionless, waiting for the shadow to reveal its identity. The candles are blown out from the breeze and I cannot make out the image. I feel the soft touch up my arm, passed my shoulders, cupping my chin and pressing its kiss into my mouth. I hear a sigh of satisfaction in my ear. I open my eyes to see nothing in front of me. Scanning the room, I can see only the few candles that remain lit. No trace of anyone is left in the room, just the sweet taste of its lips on mine. The comfort lays me back to sleep and I dream of love.

Devoted

Horrible, the end of this night is near. I wish to push back the clock and lay in bed next to you for a few more hours. The quiet slumber of being in love gives relief in our whimper or our moan. I watch as your hair clings to the side of your face and the moisture rolls down your cheek. I love to feel the heat radiate from your body while I blow cool breaths across your back. I would caress you all night until I could no longer lift my arms. Endless strides of pleasure create the taste along your lips and in between the movements. I love you long and I love you hard. I will love you when I can only love in my dreams. I have felt the moment of rich truth and struggled to stay. I pray that one day my request shall be answered and I will love you until the end of my days.

Established

For many countless days I have searched the heavens for a moment of stability. I held onto many natural things where I put my trust and faith. I found these things were only dust and shadows of a life I was waiting for. I had hoped for success in many areas; to be more distinguished, to have been remembered for deeds done and lives changed because of how I lived. I wanted to be financially successful, with more to give.; to be loved by the one who promised to cherish, not forget after the passion ended. Still I am seeking the filler to make me complete. I stumble in a daze wondering where and when I shall find my heaven. I have such fervor to find all that was promised to me. I shall not stop until I have understood all that is revealed. Soon I will rest in the knowledge of my understanding. I will live the life I was promised. I will give the love I was meant to reflect.

Passing in the Night

The night fell in a slow, endearing pace. It seemed to comfort me by the soothing sounds of all nature's creatures and motions. I walked alone in the pitch, thinking of the salty air that blew from the north. I could taste the small trace across my lips. Making my way toward the beach, I noticed a silhouette coming toward me. The pale, smooth skin shone under the silk wrap that blew to reveal her beautiful figure. As the meeting became closer and closer, I could make out faint images of her details. Her hair shimmered in deep hues of sandalwood. Her eyes of topaz seemed reflective and compassionate, as I caught a glimpse from the light of the moon. She walked in grace and elegance up the beach. I stood still in the presence of her beauty. I could not speak a word. I could only acknowledge in reverence as she passed. I watched her from a distance and imagined what it would be like to live in her world. I wanted to chase her and ask for her hand in mine. I thought better of the internal conversation and turned to catch up with the life that was my own.

Languish

Regret

If I had known this would be the last time...

...I held your body next to mine, I would have never let go.
...I kissed your lips, I would have tasted them longer.
...I gazed into your eyes, I would have seen your Love.
...I made love to you, I would have made it last until dawn.
...I tasted your sweetness, I would have taken my time.
...I felt the scratches of passion down my back, I would have never healed.
...to hear you scream my name, I would have kept the moment at its peak.
...to see you in the unchanging light, I would have never looked away.
...I told you I loved you, I would have shown you more every day.

Infinite Dismay

The breeze blows in from the east to lay frost over my soul and release a tremor of guilt. Steam rises from the burning of passion with what is left behind in the chill of autumn. I have lost the only true love I wanted to know and remember; the sweet pheromone of her freshness, the silky smooth texture of her hair, the seductive taste of her skin. I look back to the times I caressed her hips and pulled her close in sensuality. Impossible as it may seem, this reality, this hypocrisy is the truth that lies next to those who sin daily. Doubting all I have seen and trusting only what I have been told to believe, confusion mounts upon the buried option of leaving the unveiled to be spirited away to a never existing world of hope.

Destroyed

Slap me down! Finish the task! Wrench the life from my heart and kill my soul. Return those blows of rejection and hatred, never feeling the love that was there in the shadow of loneliness. Keep in mind all that has been in contemplation of a lovers' quarrel. Refusing love embedded into a relationship of life. Give hope to another along with the sweetness in a portrait of divine intervention, while leaving all else to spring into oblivion. Withholding nothing short of a damnation said to be the wholesome fate of the inner being. Kiss me goodnight and lay me to rest in the depth of my personal hell. Bury my memories with a silk ribbon to be laid on my breast. Forget Love was ever felt in the bright sunlight of youth; never recall the taste of happiness.

Broken

My heart is torn too deep to mend. I try to fill in the cracks with laughter and humor. I try to seal the wound with caring and nurturing of my children. I find empty spaces and putty in a few of the holes, but what can replace the Love that has been ripped from within? The food is no longer an option, for I have to change the nature of life and lose the weight that covered up the scar. I am taking off the layers of my guarded soul. I am bringing down the walls I have labored too many nights to build. The light shines in every now and again. The warmth feels good. I have not abandoned the idea of never loving another. I think, *just not now*. I will no longer try to poison myself with nicotine and alcohol; killing myself slowly is the easy way out. I have more to think on now instead of just my pity and my hurts. I am living again! I want to be the woman I loved in the early years of life. The woman before the hard hit of love lost twice. The wound is healing itself through the daily toil of growing and maturing. I understand I will live for today and live I shall. A broken heart can never truly mend, but it can learn to love again.

Betrayed

A flare for the fancy and a taste for revenge; consorting in devious overthrows; portraying love and kinship to uttermost deception; ramblings and mutterings of keenly devised chaos. Unsuspecting are those closest to the heart, with wide range in full view and subtle undertones of hypocrisy, these untold tales of untold deeds, only to be revealed when the masterful is undone. Oh the torturous lives we lead to that one day of full embodiment in radiance and salvation; to explain all that was conceived for the betterment of a daily peace; to control a twisted reality of honesty.

Reality

The time we spent together building our hopes and dreams was my reality. The days we shared as the first face we saw in the morning to the last we loved at night, that was my reality. The days of barely making the money stretch to give more than we ever dreamt possible, that was my reality. I have nurtured and cared for our children with such a passion, that was my reality. I have experienced our love bloom into more than a dream, that was my reality. This person I see before me is a man I have never met. I think back to who you used to be. I look for him everyday since I awoke to this bad dream of someone else's life. Today I search for ways to make this nightmare make sense to my reality. Now to let go of a love that was more to me than any reality I could have ever known, that is my tragedy.

Forgiveness

Knowing the way to your soul and the path it travels along
your body, I find my way without an upward glance. I can
see my way to your heart and capture the beat of each step.
I have felt every touch of love and endured all the pain.
Turning over in the sheets, I outwardly stare at the wall.
The night's passion was abruptly taken from the
moment of satisfaction and replaced with the tangent of
disappointment. Disdain dripped from the lips I love to kiss,
and blasphemous contempt poured from the voice that sings
me to sleep. A playful touch and yearning to last past the
unobtainable joy, I broke the stride and hurt the only high
we would experience. Give me your hand and let me show
you a road less traveled.

Longing

In the deepest part of my heart I have felt the warmth of your love. Sometimes I can hear your voice calling out to me in random daily events. I look for you in every face or in every smile I encounter. I remember the smell of your fragrance. I close my eyes to imagine the look you would give me when you were in the mood. Most days I keep busy to let my mind rest. If I am idle the thoughts of missing you come flooding in and overtake me. I hope that wherever you may be, you are doing well. It has been said, "It is better to have loved and lost then to have never loved before." I don't know as that I would agree with those who say this. If they had ever loved you as I have, they would think again.

Dreams

Midnight comes, a swift chill of a crisp, December night. Turning back the covers of the king-sized bed; loneliness was never felt so strongly. Entering sleep was hardly accomplished with ease. I could hear the rhythms of the night. The sounds of the trees made it difficult to fall asleep. The continuous traffic humming from the nearby highway would not allow my mind to rest. The coolness of the sheets made my body tense and unable to relax. I remained still long enough to heat one spot I would lay for the night. I found myself intrigued by the writing of a Latin poet that could touch the heart of any woman and make her feel love instantly. As I read each romantic verse, I saw you standing in the doorway. My eyes soon became blinded by my tears. A lump was formed in my throat and I couldn't speak. I just smiled and invited you to share the warmth of my small spot. I held onto you all night and whispered the verse of passion and promise into your ear. We lay side by side, dreaming of heaven. My dream took me to the jade forests of Asia and I entered the peace that comes from eternal love. I awoke to an empty bed and a cold pillow. Years later, I thought of you and wondered where your dream took you.

Sanctified

My misfortunes lead me to a life of undoubting shame. Though I passed the days in a flash of time, a blur of mist and fog, I found my way through the forest of jade. I turn my cheek. The moisture falls in a blanket of haze, leaving my vision in a dull, grey color. Your body resembled the stoic grace of elegance. A melancholy mood weaved its way through empathy and strife, revealing solitude in such empty hollows of reality. Poised toward heaven I am waiting for my carriage home. I stare into the sapphire sky and catch the brilliant sparkle of light in the shroud. The motions dance in the darkness, bought by joy and peace. I soar high in the midnight, leaving behind the morbid death to play out its role in a life well spent; no tears, no sorrow, no ill-conceived notion, just the peace of passion. I have no unknown complexities. I have survived the torment of betrayal. All that hinders me now falls to the ground in ashes. I am reborn.

Solitude

In moments of turmoil I look for the door and wonder if I should step out or close it softly. Do I face the Giant that stands before me? Or do I cower in agony and wait for the blast of hell? In my most desperate situation I hope to plan for the next coming day that can only seen by living a life of not knowing tomorrow. In fear of making the wrong decision I turn the handle and peek out into the pitch of night. I feel the stinging rain and a cold chill covers my body. I am left empty. Nothing left to warm me or fill my soul wit love. I begin to sob and wail for an event unimaginably out of reach. I fall to sleep from the tears and the tense grip I have around my knees. Please rock me to peaceful dreams. I yearn for the sunrise of a solution to the pain I have befriended.

Leaving

Just past the midnight hour I feel for you next to me and an empty space was all that slid through my fingers. I know the evening was unexpected and a little distant in the conversations of hope. I left with the realization I was to never return to love so warm. The morning came too soon and the night passed too quickly. I hadn't the chance to experience all your love had to offer. I felt the need to bring more to your feet and lay down all I could be. I hadn't the notion to need more than what you could possibly desire. I wanted only your happiness. I watched you slumber in peaceful dreams, I took my last kiss, and closed this life behind me.

LaVergne, TN USA
07 January 2010
169121LV00005B/24/P